H

By Mandy Cleeve
Designed by Gary Cookson
Cover design by Robert Perry

KINGFISHER
An imprint of Larousse plc
Elsley House,
24-30 Great Titchfield Street,
London, W1P 7AD

First published by Larousse plc 1996

2 4 6 8 10 9 7 5 3

ISBN 0 7534 0075 8

Kingfisher

WHAT IS AN INSECT?

The world is swarming with insects – the most common animal group on Earth. Scientists have counted at least a million different species, although thousands of new kinds are found every year!

INSECTS EVERYWHERE!

Minibeasts range in size from tiny mites that are barely visible to giant beetles the size of a human hand. But not all bugs are insects. All *true* insects have six legs and three body parts. Most have wings and all have a hard outer skeleton that protects their soft insides. Insects hatch their young from eggs.

WE'RE GOING TO DO A SCHOOL PROJECT TODAY!

BOO!

YAY!

ON INSECTS!

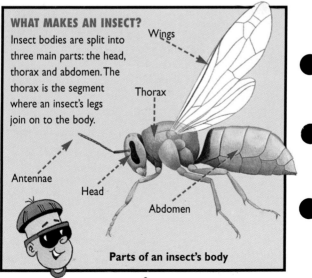

WHAT MAKES AN INSECT?

Insect bodies are split into three main parts: the head, thorax and abdomen. The thorax is the segment where an insect's legs join on to the body.

Wings

Thorax

Antennae

Head

Abdomen

Parts of an insect's body

amazing fact

Eight out of ten of all creatures are creepy crawlies!

This spider may be a little horror, but it's *not* an insect! It has eight legs, not six, and only two body parts.

HOW DOES AN INSECT SEE?

THE COMPOUND EYE

An insect eye is made up of thousands of tiny lenses that combine to give a mosaic picture of the world. This means that although their vision is not very detailed, bugs can see in lots of directions at the same time.

ALMOST AS POWERFUL AS MINE!

INSECT FACTS

- Insects are invertebrates – so they have no backbone.
- For every human being alive there are at least 200 million minibeasts. Phew!

- Insects live everywhere except in the oceans.
- Insects were the first animals to roam the Earth. Fish followed them 100 million years later.

3

4

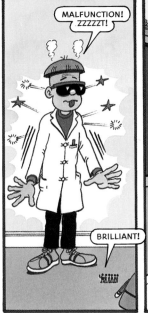

5

BUGS IN THE SCHOOL

The Bash Street Kids are used to seeing bugs, flies and fleas in the school. But now they've been shrunk, they'll discover what gruesome habits these little pests really have!

GHASTLY GERM SPREADERS

All these minibeasts like to make their homes indoors. While house flies feed on our food and rubbish, some bugs and fleas survive on the blood of human beings and pets! Germs are spread as these insects buzz from meal to meal.

BLUEBOTTLE

There are at least 90,000 different types of fly, but this bluebottle might be the most familiar. Its speed and excellent eyesight make it very difficult to catch.

HOW DOES A FLY EAT?

The fly has taste buds on its feet, so its stamps all over its dinner before eating it! Then it squirts out saliva to mash the food into liquid. Finally the fly sucks up the meal through its long, thin mouth.

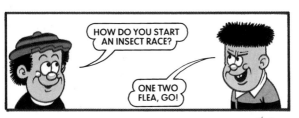

HOW DO YOU START AN INSECT RACE?

ONE TWO FLEA, GO!

HOW DOES A FLY WALK UPSIDE DOWN?

Flies have tiny claws and suction pads on their feet to allow them to cling to walls. As they land, flies grasp on to the ceiling and flip their bodies upside down!

WHAT IS A BUG?

Bugs look similar to beetles, except they have a flat, dull back. They also have a sharp beak that they use like a straw to pierce and suck up food. Beware – bugs can give a nasty bite!

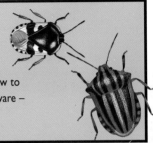

FACTS ABOUT FLEAS

These tiny parasites live off the blood of large mammals. Fleas aren't able to fly, but they are expert jumpers. Wilfrid can't compete with his pogo stick – a flea can easily leap over 100 times its own body height!

PESKY FLEA!

amazing fact

A hungry flea can perform 600 leaps in an hour!

7

BILLIONS OF BEETLES

> ONE IN EVERY THREE ANIMALS IS A BEETLE, AND, SINCE *I'M* NOT . . .

One out of every three creatures is a beetle – including the common ladybird! These tough little monsters are covered in a thick layer of armour hiding a pair of filmy wings underneath.

BOMBARDIER BEETLE

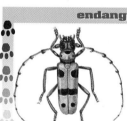

Although just a centimetre long, this beetle has a ferocious weapon to scare off enemies. It sprays its attackers with a burning liquid that explodes with a loud bang!

endangered species

Although there are over 400,000 kinds of beetle, many are disappearing forever. This beautiful rosalia longhorn beetle has been hunted for so long that it is now very rare.

DUNG BEETLE

This beetle is pushing home its favourite meal – fresh, steaming dung! It will lay eggs in the ball and bury it so its young will have a meal ready when they hatch out.

BEES **AND** WASPS

In summer the air can seem alive with the drone of bees and wasps, buzzing amongst the flowers. But their stripes carry a warning for Smiffy: I can hurt you, so don't touch!

I'VE GOT TWO BEES!

THAT'S WHY I'M IN CLASS 2B!

The bumblebee drinks the flower's nectar through its long tube-shaped mouth. Then it brushes pollen into special baskets on its back legs, to take back to the hive.

AWAY!

A bee can only sting once in its life – it has a barbed sting that stays stuck in its victim. Wasps are hunters, so they have a smooth sting that they can use time after time.

HOMEMADE HOMES

Some bees and wasps live alone, but most are 'social' insects. While bees usually make hives out of wax, wasps live in nests crafted out of pulped wood or mud. This paper wasp nest was started by a queen with thin layers of chewed up wood or 'paper'. Inside the nest are dozens of hexagonal cells – miniature nurseries where the young wasps are hatched.

DIFFERENCES BETWEEN BEES AND WASPS

- Bees are stocky insects with furry bodies.
- Wasps have thin waists and little hair.
- Bees are strictly vegetarian bugs. They use their long tongues to drink nectar.
- Wasps are ferocious meat-eaters, with powerful jaws for chewing their prey.

- Bees gather pollen to make honey and wax.
- There are only two types of wasp that make honey.
- Bees fly in swarms.
- Wasps never swarm.
- Bees are usually peaceful, only stinging in defence.
- Wasps use their sting as a weapon to kill their food.

11

BUTTERFLIES AND MOTHS

Butterflies and moths are easily the best-looking bugs. Their four wings are covered with tiny overlapping scales that form fantastic patterns of colour.

FROM EGG TO ADULT

These insects have to endure four massive changes before they grow up. Moths and butterflies all have to move from egg, to caterpillar, to chrysalis before they reach adulthood!

WHY DID THE BREAD ROLL?

BECAUSE IT SAW THE BUTTER FLY!

WHAT'S THE DIFFERENCE?

There are actually *more* kinds of moth than butterfly, but moths seem rarer because they are often more active at night. Moths usually have plump, hairy bodies and dull wings. Butterflies are bright creatures with thin waists.

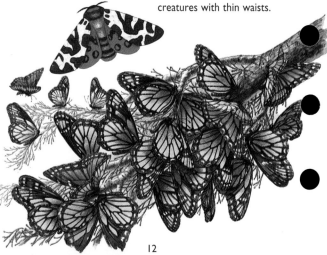

LONG LEGS FOR LEAPING

Grasshoppers and crickets are very closely related – just like Toots and Sidney, the Bash Street twins. Both types of minibeast have long, super-powerful legs. Grasshoppers can easily jump over a metre in the air! Look at the antennae to tell them apart: grasshopper feelers are much shorter than those of the cricket.

IT'S CRICKET WITH A CRICKET!

amazing fact

Locusts are very large tropical grasshoppers that travel in swarms of more than 50 billion!

THE BUG MUSICIAN

Male grasshoppers and crickets make a loud, chirping sound to attract females and scare off rivals. Crickets produce their song by rubbing their front wings together. Grasshoppers make sound in a similar way to a musician playing the violin. They use their legs like a violinist's bow to produce grasshopper music from ridged veins on their front wings!

BUSY ANTS

Can you imagine how many ants and termites are alive today? It's an impossible task – there are more of these little horrors than any other creature on Earth! Ants are highly organized social insects.

ANT SOCIETY

Every ant colony revolves around a single queen ant who lays all of the eggs. The other insects are workers. It is their job to gather food, clean the nest and nurse the queen's babies. Special soldier ants with large jaws spend their lives guarding the nest.

LET'S VISIT SOME ANTS!

I'VE GOT AN AUNT DORIS!

INSIDE THE MINI CITY

Ants build nests by tunnelling underground or piling up leaves or soil to make mounds. These fascinating insect houses have special rooms for lots of different things – there are larders, nurseries and even rubbish chambers! An average colony could be home for more than 100,000 ants.

ARMY ANTS

Rainforest army ants have no fixed home. Instead they roam the forest floor in huge swarms, devouring *anything* in their path.

ANT PARTNERSHIPS

The large blue butterfly has a special relationship with one type of ant. When these bugs find the butterfly's caterpillars they 'milk' them like cows! The ants extract a fluid that they feed to their young.

LEAF-CUTTER ANTS

These minibeasts are the gardeners of the insect world. They tear off pieces of leaves and bring them back to the nest. The leaves are often bigger than the bugs themselves – the equivalent of a man carrying a small car home! At the nest the ants chew the greenery and mix it with saliva to create compost. Spotty would be amazed to learn that the leafcutters then use this homemade soil to grow their food – fungus.

WONDER IF THE ANTS WOULD CUT THIS UP?

HOMEWORK

15

THE MEGA-LEGGERS!

Some creepy crawlies are not the insects that they appear to be. In fact, woodlice are more closely related to crabs than insects! And centipedes and millipedes have far too many legs to even qualify.

TIMID LITTLE HORRORS

These minibeasts have one thing in common – a love of damp hiding places. Woodlice cannot survive anywhere else. Their shells aren't waterproof, so they would die if they dried out!

HOPE I DON'T SPRAIN AN ANKLE!

WOODLOUSE FACTS

- Woodlice have 14 legs – seven on each side.
- They carry their babies in pouches just like kangaroos.
- Woodlice moult in two stages – one half at a time.
- Woodlice are *crustaceans* – a type of animal that has a hard, jointed body and legs. Woodlice are one of the only crustaceans that don't live in the ocean.

SELF-DEFENCE

When threatened, woodlice roll into a ball, so their soft undersides are protected by their armoured body plates.

CENTIPEDE AND MILLIPEDE FACTS

These multi-limbed bugs come from the *arthropod* family, which means 'jointed legs'. Some species have over 300 – at least 15 times more than all the Bash Street gang's legs added together!

CENTIPEDES

Centipedes are fast-moving minibeasts that are most active at night. They are speedy predators that hunt insects and other small creatures. To identify one, look at its legs – centipedes only have one pair on each body segment.

WHAT GOES 99 CLUNK?

A CENTIPEDE WITH A WOODEN LEG!

amazing fact

The biggest centipede is a 46-legged goliath that lives in South America. It is 25cm long and 2.5 thick!

MILLIPEDES

Millipedes are slow, peaceful vegetarians. They all have two pairs of short, strong legs per body segment.

SLUGS AND SNAILS

There are an amazing 70,000 kinds of slug and snail – some even live in the sea! Their soft bodies earn them a place in the mollusc family.

BUG COUSINS

Slugs are actually snail relatives that have lost their shells. They get around on a wide muscular foot, leaving a trail of slime that helps them slide over jagged surfaces more easily.

WHAT IS A SNAIL?

A snail spends its life inside a hard spiral shell. If it is threatened, it retreats into its mobile home and seals the opening up with slime that dries into a hard cap.

WHAT IS A SLUG?

A slug has thick leathery skin which is covered in mucus to stop it drying out.

HOW DO THEY EAT?

Slugs and snails have rows and rows of tiny teeth on their tongues called *radula*. They use their radula to scoop up their food and shred it.

IT'S PLUG ON A SLUG!

Most land slugs are plant-eaters, but some hunt worms and even other slugs!

WRIGGLY WORMS

There are hundreds of types of worm. Although some are very simple animals, others have bodies that are made up of tiny segments.

LONG AND LEGLESS

As they have no legs or wings, worms travel by moving their bodies in waves – up to ten a minute. They make tunnels for themselves by swallowing earth. As the soil is full of tiny pieces of dead leaves, the worms can have a meal at the same time!

WHAT DOES THIS SPAGHETTI REMIND YOU OF?

The leech can swell to ten times its weight in one meal!

PARASITES

Some species of worm are parasites that live off other animals and humans. Leeches have suckers that pierce the skin, so they can gorge off blood. Tapeworms secure themselves inside the intestines, living off the food that passes through.

This pork tapeworm grows to over four metres long.

EARTHWORMS

Earthworms are helpful to gardeners because they mix air into the soil as they burrow along.

amazing fact

A full-size whale tapeworm can grow up to 30m long!

SPIDERS AND SCORPIONS

Although Plug and Wilfrid are terrified of spiders and scorpions, over 98 per cent of them are harmless. In fact, more people are hurt by bees and wasps than spiders!

AMAZING ARACHNIDS

These tough little hunters are members of the *arachnid* family – a group that includes ticks and mites. Unlike insects, they all have eight walking legs, just two body parts and no wings or antennae. Spiders have eight eyes, but as they don't have compound vision they are very short-sighted!

HERE WE ARE BESIDE THE ZOO INSECTS. I'M SCARED OF SPIDERS!

DON'T WORRY! THE SCORPIONS WILL GET YOU FIRST!

HAIRY WEB-WEAVERS

Spiders are famous for their intricate silk webs which are both beautiful and incredibly strong. A large spider's web can contain at least 30 metres of silk, but rarely weighs more than half of a milligram! This garden spider will spin a new wheel-shaped web every day. When an insect gets trapped in the sticky threads the spider quickly ties it up with more silk to stop it escaping.

WHAT IS A TARANTULA?

This name is often used for big, hairy spiders like this one. But these mini-monsters are actually called 'bird-eating spiders'. Real tarantulas are very small, venomous, European spiders.

UGLY BEAST!

SCORPIONS

These arachnids live in hot, dry regions, hidden from sight under rocks and stones. They feed at night, crushing and tearing their prey with fearsome claws. If the victim struggles, it is paralysed instantly by a quick stab from the scorpion's poisonous tail.

FUNNEL WEB

This funnel web spider is one of the most venomous arachnids alive. Watch out – it's also one of the few spiders to have fangs big enough to pierce human flesh!

amazing fact

The webs of the nephila spider are so strong that people have used them to make fishing nets!

HOW MANY SPIDERS?

There are at least 35,000 kinds of spider, living everwhere except Antarctica.

EXOTIC INSECTS

The Bash Street Kids will see some of the most amazing creepy crawlies in the zoo insect house. Even Plug looks normal compared to this gallery of bug horrors!

GIRAFFE WEEVIL

It's easy to see how the giraffe weevil got its name – its neck is twice as long as its body! This fantastic beetle lives in the rainforests of Madagascar, nodding its great neck as a warning if threatened by other males.

STICK INSECT

This stick insect is a real camouflage expert. It is almost impossible to spot as it sits motionless in trees – it even sways in the wind just like a real twig! These curious minibeasts mainly inhabit the tropical regions of Asia.

WHAT WEIRD LOOKING CREATURES!

LOOK WHO'S TALKING!

TARANTULA

This famous type of wolf spider may have a nasty reputation, but it's actually a very shy creature. The tarantula comes from southern Europe, where it likes to live in burrows, darting out of its home to catch passing bugs.

BRILLIANT BUGS AT RISK

The most fantastic bugs of all come from the world's tropical rainforests. These places receive huge amounts of warmth, sunlight and rain, encouraging the most colourful and massive creepy crawlies to develop. Yet every day enormous areas of rainforest are being destroyed. Many wonderful species of insect are at risk of dying out as their home disappears.

More insects live in the rainforest than anywhere else on Earth. This blue morpho butterfly can't survive if this rich habitat is wiped out.

SCARY STAG BEETLE

European stag beetles fight ferocious bug battles, using their enormous jaws to throw opponents on to the floor. Sometimes the mouthparts of these wrestlers are bigger than their bodies!

amazing fact

A stag beetle can grow to over 10cm in length!

RECORD-BREAKERS

Insects are all animal champions – there are more of these little horrors than any other creature on Earth. But which are the bug record-breakers?

FROM BIGGEST AND SMALLEST

Insects are usually small creatures, but the minute fairy fly is in a league of it own! This microscopic marvel is too tiny to see properly – it's even smaller than a full stop.

HERE ARE OUR RECORD BREAKING KIDS! GUESS WHAT RECORDS THEY BREAK!

A) UNLOVELIEST
B) UNCLEVEREST
C) UNFOCUSEDEST

THE WORLD'S WIDEST

The gigantic Australian hercules emperor moth is the broadest insect in the world. With its fat, hairy body and enormous wings it measures over 28 centimetres across! This huge record breaker has another amazing claim to fame. The male moth is equipped with fantastic feather-like antennae that can smell passing females. Using these, the moth can pick up the scents of female moths that are over 11 kilometres away!

WHICH IS THE BIGGEST BUTTERFLY?

Birdwings are the most enormous butterflies on Earth. From a distance, they might be mistaken for birds – they fly very slowly, flapping their long wings up and down. The Queen Alexandra birdwing has the longest wing span of all, stretching over 25 centimetres from tip to tip! This rare and beautiful creature can only be found in the rainforests of Papua New Guinea.

INSECT HEAVYWEIGHT

The goliath beetle is easily the heaviest member of the insect family. Adult males can tip the scales at over 100 grams! This little monster is also one of the biggest beetles there is – sometimes measuring over 15 centimetres long.

GIANT EARTHWORM

The South African giant earthworm dwarfs all other worms. It can grow up to seven metres long, with a body at least three centimetres thick!

amazing fact

The biggest Antarctic inland animal is a wingless fly measuring about 60mm long!

27

BUG BABIES

Although Danny and Plug are children, they look very similar to adult humans. However some young bugs have to go through many amazing changes of appearance before they grow up!

CREEPY CRAWLY CHILDREN

Insects lay eggs which, when they hatch, produce larvae. Many bugs change shape several times before they become adults, but not all develop like this. When some minibeasts are born, they already look like miniature versions of their parents.

WHAT A LOVELY BUTTERFLY!

DREAM ON, PLUG!

HOW BUTTERFLIES GROW

This remarkable bug life cycle is called *metamorphosis*. First, the female butterfly lays some eggs on a nearby plant. The eggs soon hatch into hungry caterpillars. After a few weeks each bug wraps itself in a silk cocoon and hangs upside down. Inside this capsule, the caterpillar's body is totally transformed. Finally, a creased, but fully grown butterfly emerges.

A growing caterpillar will munch through thousands of times its own weight in leaves!

28

WOLF SPIDER

This wolf spider has a very clever method of looking after her eggs – they are carried along in a specially woven silk rucksack! When they hatch, the young leap on to the safety of their mother's back.

SCORPION BABIES

Scorpions don't lay eggs – they give birth to live young. The tiny newborns are pale and helpless creatures with soft bodies. The mother carries all her babies on her back, only letting them climb down to feed. After a few weeks they shed their skins, to reveal fully developed scorpion bodies.

EARWIG

This minibeast must be the best of all bug mothers. The female earwig closely guards her eggs all winter, keeping them warm and licking them clean.

The young butterfly stretches out in the sunlight to dry out its crinkled wings.

INSECT HOMES

Insects need to live somewhere safe and close to food. But lots of bugs don't have a real home, instead they use their nests as a place to breed their young before moving on.

SOCIAL BUGS AND LITTLE LONERS

Some minibeasts prefer to live in huge colonies, building elaborate nests that will survive for generations. Others live alone in all kinds of nests, dens and burrows.

TRAPDOOR SPIDER

This resourceful arachnid uses its house as a clever trap for catching prey. The specially built front door of its burrow has a silk hinge so that it can be opened and shut easily. In the night, the spider hides in the tunnel with the door slightly ajar. When it hears bug footsteps it bursts out of the tunnel and ambushes its prey. The spider injects its victim with venom before dragging it back down to be eaten.

TERMITE MUD-MOUNDS

Termites are the greatest insect architects in the world. They construct towering homes from soil, saliva and droppings – some can stand over six metres high! Millions of termites live together inside these complex structures.

WEAVER ANTS

These little horrors choose to dwell in homemade tents made of stitched foliage. The ants hold their young larvae in their mouths and push them through the leaves. As they are weaved in and out, the grubs produce a sticky, silk thread that firmly binds the nest together.

BRILLIANT BEEHIVES

Wild honey bees are social insects that live in holes in rocks and trees. But if a bee-keeper offers them a ready-built nest box, or hive, they are quite happy to move in!

Inside the new hive the bees build hundreds of rooms called cells out of a special kind of wax.

LIFE IN THE POND

Visit your local pond and discover an incredible variety of insect wildlife! Ponds are carefully balanced communities teeming with tiny creatures.

WATER BUGS

Some creepy crawlies spend their whole lives in ponds and streams, each species adopting its own unique way of getting around and finding food. Yet others only visit the water during certain seasons of the year. Spring is the busiest time in the pond, when most young bugs are born.

DRAGONFLY

Many little horrors spend their youth in freshwater. Dragonfly nymphs live under the surface for at least a year. When the time is right, they climb out into the sunlight – splitting their skin to reveal a fully grown dragonfly, ready to dart off into the air.

FANCY A DIP, SMIFFY?

NOPE! I HAD A BATH LAST YEAR!

INSECT POOL

34

35

KEEPING IN TOUCH

Insects don't chat like Fatty and 'Erbert – they have their own methods of getting the message across! Some bugs rely on antennae to communicate, whilst others use special movements and signals.

MINIBEAST COMMUNICATION

Creepy crawlies need to communicate with each other for lots of reasons – it might be to attract mates, scare off predators or seek out food. The main sense organs for most bugs are the antennae, feelers that they use to taste and smell and touch.

FATTY TO 'ERBERT!

MOTH MESSAGES

Moths use their feathery feelers to send scent signals to each other in the dark. Male moths can smell females many kilometres away.

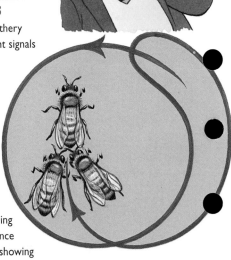

DANCING BEES

When a honey bee finds food it tells the others in the hive by performing a unique circular dance on the honeycomb showing the direction of the meal.

FIREFLY

This remarkable creature is actually a kind of beetle that can produce light in its abdomen. A chemical reaction takes place inside the firefly, allowing it to switch the light on and off whenever it wants. The wingless females flash in the dark in order to attract males flying above in the night sky.

I'M PICKING YOU UP ON MY ANTENNAS!

COCKROACH

This scavenging beetle is a night creature – scuttling around trying to find food. As it is too dark to see, this little horror totally depends upon its long, quivering antennae to guide it. If danger approaches, the cockroach's feelers pick up the change in air currents and it hides until it's safe to come out.

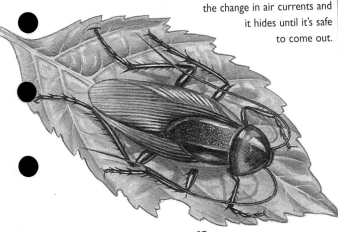

MINI HUNTERS

Plug the praying mantis looks funny, but being a bug hunter is very serious business. Many minibeasts have to kill in order to survive.

PINT-SIZED PREDATORS

Some minibeasts set up ambushes to surprise their prey, whilst others rely on strength and speed. The victim must react quickly or it's doomed to be another bug's dinner.

SPIDER WEBS

When an insect stumbles into the spider's sticky trap, the arachnid quickly pounces and wraps its prey in silk thread. Inside the parcel, the victim's body melts to a soup that the spider drinks up later.

amazing fact

A spider's web is as strong as steel of the same thickness!

FLOWER MANTIS

This kind of praying mantis looks almost invisible as it perches on the flower. It holds its powerful forearms in a praying position – ready to grasp hold of any unsuspecting insects that might land nearby.

CAMOUFLAGE AND DEFENCE

With so many skilful hunters about, creepy crawlies need to protect themselves. Every day bugs face being attacked and eaten by predators.

KEEPING OUT OF DANGER

Some insects rely on making a quick getaway if danger comes near. Others prefer to face their attackers head on and fight back. Clever bugs use camouflage to trick their enemies.

HERE'S SOME SELF DEFENCE!

PEACOCK BUTTERFLY

The wing pattern of this peacock butterfly looks just like a pair of startling eyes – sure to scare off any bird!

WOOD ANTS

These angry bugs scare off intruders by spraying them with a hot, stinging liquid, fired out from the ant's abdomen.

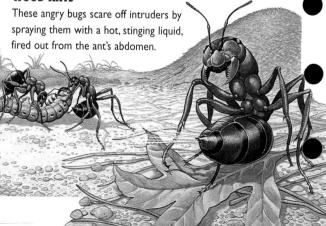

PEPPERED MOTH

This ingenious little creature has evolved into two forms – one light and one dark. The dark peppered moth has developed in industrial areas. Its shady colour helps it camouflage itself against smoke-blackened trees.

HOVERFLY

The harmless hoverfly wears the wasp's black and yellow coat so predators are tricked into thinking that it carries a nasty sting.

LEAF INSECT

This minibeast is a master of disguise, impossible to spot as it sits motionless in the trees. The leaf insect even has raised lines on its body like the veins on a *real* leaf. This clever bug is careful only to move and feed at night when it knows it can't be seen.

FRIEND OR FOE?

Insects do some useful jobs – such as collecting rubbish and encouraging new plants to grow. But not all are human friends. In fact some should be avoided!

LITTLE PESTS AND HUMAN HELPERS

Some minibeasts can cause all kinds of problems. But before we blame the bugs, we should think about how we treat *them* – people can be pests too! Humans are responsible for wiping out whole species of insect and destroying their homes.

HOW MANY PESTS CAN YOU SPOT HERE?

ANSWER

CORRECT! NINE, OF COURSE!

MOSQUITO

Some mosquitos can carry a fatal disease called malaria that kills about one million people every year.

COLORADO BEETLE

The colorado beetle and its larvae can eat through whole fields of potato plants in days. This stripey bug will also devour tomato and tobacco crops.

LOCUST

Of all the insects in the world, the locust causes the most damage to humans beings. As it migrates in gigantic swarms, it strips every crop field in its path. The locust's rampages can result in famine and starvation on a devastating scale.

DEATH'S HEAD HAWKMOTH

This serious pest has a skull-like marking on its back. The moth's hungry caterpillars like to dine on potato crops.

NATURE'S HELPERS

Bees pollinate plants and give us honey.

Ladybirds help humans by eating the caterpillars and aphids that attack garden plants.

BURYING BEETLE

This creepy crawly spends its life scuttling about in search of dead animals. When the beetle finds a corpse, it buries it and lays some eggs nearby. Later, the hatched larvae will feed on the dead matter – clearing away nature's rubbish and making the soil more fertile at the same time!

44

45

Sidney's Project

Snails leave a trail of slime behind them to help them to move. I left a trail of slime behind me when I fell into Rasher's pig sty last week

← me

Plug's Project

A praying Mantis is an insect which holds its front legs as if it were praying. Which is good because if it waved its front legs it would be a waving Mantis and the little insects it eats would see it waving and run away and praying Mantises would become extinct and I'd have nothing to write about.

Spotty's Project

Lady Birds aren't ladies or birds — they're BEETLES! Gardeners like them 'cos they eat garden pests. I like them kos they've got lots of SPOTS!

Smiffy's Project

WE all got shrunk so WE could study insects. Even MY brane brain got shrunk to the size of a PEA! What's new? asks Teacher. Insects have got SIX legs — like Me and my MUM and DAD — not each. togETHER.

STOP! I DO NOT UNDERSTAND THIS SILLINESS. SIGNED TECHNO.

GO BUG-SPOTTING!

You don't have to shrink down in size to study bugs properly. If you look carefully you'll find that the world is teeming with all kinds of minibeasts.

THE SMALLEST ANIMALS

Some creepies that live near humans are almost too tiny to see without a magnifying glass. This minute silverfish is a harmless insect that can be found lurking in kitchen cupboards – one blink and you'll miss it!

LIVING WITH BUGS

Houses provide minibeasts with good hunting grounds and ideal nesting places. Look out for flies in the kitchen and house spiders trapped in the bath!

HOW TO OBSERVE MINIBEASTS

 Do look in the garden – it's always rich in bug life.

 Do think before you touch as some insects can bite.

 Don't keep bugs as pets – they're happier in the wild.

 Don't forget to wash your hands after handling bugs.

Be kind to creepy crawlies – To them you're a giant!